# NEW YORK

BY
LUCAS HUNT

NEW YORK
THANE & PROSE
2022

Published by Thane & Prose, New York

First Edition

*Book cover and interior design by Lynn Rawden*
*Cover typeset in Bodoni Old Face, interior pages typeset in Bembo*
*Cover Photograph by Lerone Pieters*
ISBN 978-0- 5783590-9-0

How many dawns, chill from his rippling rest
The seagull's wings shall dip and pivot him,
Shedding white rings of tumult, building high
Over the chained bay waters Liberty—

—"To Brooklyn Bridge," by Hart Crane

To Annie

# CONTENTS

City of smoke and steam
I do not know what you mean,
the fog is thick and white,
streets are full of life.

# EMPIRE STATE

Sing the spring chorus of muses,
tower elite, flowering avenues
support a pageantry of small feet,
wings fly, immerse windows
in light and let fervent rain
water budding parks, fingers of grass
massage nude backs and bed the lovers—
ode to you unending patient city,
celebrate angels, outsoar catacomb
subway terminals to mount steep stairwell
with satanic energy, a crowded
street and sidewalk, elevated oneness,
high the sun of summer skies above us.

# NEVER THE SAME

My best is yet to come
what was today
happened
every little light
means hours
before tomorrow.

Were it anywhere else
it would not be
such chaos
combines to form
movements
of door and train.

Garbage fragments
float over a new river
because the water
here is never
the same as yesterday.

# OUR WEALTH

They came from the sea to find liberty
and began with bold assertion—
flight was possible before we knew it,
bay water wrapped Ellis Island,
thousands, tens of thousands, hundreds
of thousands, gray and wet,
braved all the world for America.

Here you are Mark set to go through town—
aisle of windows and steel skeletons,
to run beyond stony parks and squares,
to lift legs higher than The Empire
and race upward,
                    to fly erect
pounding pavement to oblivion,
contact ultimate, cavalry of flesh
that bounds around sharp
protruding corners of the world,
regards steep falls from palace walls and lives.

Severe terrain defines the capital
and hurdles here are evidence,
proof balloons the eye
with a fascinating principle—brave heights
and dreams made manifest in gothic realm.

Wide buildings veer the course, steer the grid
        for chaotic crowds who
cross long buckled oceans for the thrill
        of pulsing elevations,
perhaps they spot nude spectacles
        and stay forever...
            down avenue and street,

a perfect place inside
tense viscera of skin, past balconies
of cheering women and men,
forward through imaginary tapes of time,
there was never an end that was not
   a beginning.
               Here the gun sounds,
eternal races overflow curb
and sidewalk, fill my soul with certain stuff
                     that life will always be.

# DAY WILL COME

Expect the emptiness to be filled
just in time, a crane soars
over the East River,
downtown view eclipsed,
Williamsburg Bridge gone.
Then concrete, orange plastic
and swirling pigeons.
The symbol of our
world is an empty lot.
I watch a tower transcend
and wonder what earth
would say about it—
does she want architecture?
What was, is no more,
abandoned places are amusing.

And wait for whispers of the miracle come
As strange side-walkers exchange awkward glances,
Lucky couples stride hand in hand and laugh
    because night is a blackbird,
Unrecognizable faces appear from straightedge corners,
    building blocks, steel fire escapes
And iron grates in tar patched roads,
Mothers carry babies home to hard working fathers
    who dream of bigger apartments
And vacation on southern shores with frozen drinks,
People accidentally run into each other causing
    a chain reaction of bumps
And excuse me, sorry, I keep stumbling
On a name from someone else's conversation.

# HE TO HER

Columns of light
on the river
ride home
particles mix
drown
the bridge
does not move
one body
to the next
hearts forgive
hearts
beat without
thought
answer the call
if you cry
alone at night
I will comfort you.

# BAKERY

Loaves on display, the window
a warm bed of future energy,
dough risen and baked
for cheese, vegetables, mustard;
the soul's content is food.

What amorous arms of wheat,
the rolls, muffins, cookies
and cake, salty and sweet
butter cream frosting decorates
pastry of all imagination.

Hunger and dreams, milky
rivers of soon to be flesh.
Bread a staple, bread the staff
to walk up street, hill
and mountains of meat.

# WILLIAMSBURG BRIDGE

You grip handlebars
to ease the effort,
boats maneuver
subway trains climb
the center, traffic slides
on feather wheels
the compound quickness
of everything clicks,
the bridge moves
unmoved by water,
everything passes
thousands of lives
their souls transported
by the distance
and wind-blown waves
fearless of the fall,
plummets don't phase
you the bridge may
collapse in water,
beds of garbage,
skyscraper dreams,
high in many ways we
are in this shit together.

# GEORGE'S SANDWICHES

Of all the things to see or touch in Midtown
I keep returning to the sandwich story.
It goes like this: there was a young man who
took vows of poverty and every night
Grand Central station became his foundation.
George handed sandwiches to homeless people
and listened to their cares, he started there,
anyone who is generous will tell
you that change starts somewhere. It goes
beyond the turquoise painted ceiling,
Campbell Apartments, a pop-up Tiffany,
(although we're mad about commercial glory
and sculpture bursting pediment)
remember his sandwiches—I'm late to work.

# FOR JESSICA

Fuck life the actress says,
we laugh, what do you expect
from nihilists who breathe the dust
of cat shit, cocky roaches, rats—

why do you want to love?
Show me a man full of passion
then examine his closet.
Morning wind touches your skin

something beyond words—
the candle knocks against a lamp,
texture of toast crumbs on the table,
fallen hair and scalp flakes,

bamboo sunglasses, rainbow coffee
mug of room-temperature water.
Your name is on the envelope,
everything on the table.

# MAN WITH A HORN

He plays "Unforgettable"
with a flick and flutter
of polished brass,
blows music,
invisible echoes,
a soul amid machines.
A doleful tune
light as spirit,
impulsive spirals fill
my eyes.
Play my friend
back to life,
sing her voice
into my heart.
I put a twenty
in his trumpet case
in memory of you
and put life before work.

# PARKING

A siren on a shady street
sounds underwater.
What does it want now?
It's no ambulance
just a get out the way
signal to everyone.
Air conditioning
makes the moment
tolerable and knowing
this is impermanent.
The traffic, garbage,
pavement baking,
summer Friday crowd,
grocery backpack,
delivery bike, sidewalk,
parking lot app,
writing in a notebook
in my car, and helicopter.
All this is impermanent.

# THE BRIGHT FLOW

Tonight may be the best night of your life
on stage before a talkative crowd;
Manhattan skyline, river flowing strong,
massive tent protecting us from rain,
Mayor Bloomberg welcomes donors back
to Pier Two for another black-tie ball.
Tradition errors, innovation wins,
our parks are places for the past to grow
into better things, tidal estuaries
receive the ocean's gift of absolution,
kids learn about the land and architecture
before it's too late, else we destroy
our home for further profit.
Just as you stood to see the sun, we stand.

# TOLL THE CITY BELLS

There comes an hour when time no longer matters,
When sun lights building sides beyond the river
    and park, trees, water, architecture—
All appear as elements of one colossal being.

Then iron hammers ding upon a shell,
    ding reverberating waves
Of heavy sound that trembles and falls,
    ding hungry pulsing hearts
That echo through the atmosphere,
    ding violence melts away—
Even the most intense thing dissipates.

Soon church choirs will sing and hum
    omens of cloud passing above,
That ride the air on seraphic wings
    high over hill and boulevard.
And as the final embers of fire die
    when no longer fed dry wood—
There is a rage dissolved in silence.

Then the ding fades into evening
And floods of afterwork traffic fill the streets,
People hurry home from the adventure
    through a decadent maze of life—
Home to family and friends, home to love again.

# CEREMONY FOR RAISA

As I commit to the word she sings
to a flame, dips the flower in still water
and shakes it over fruit, slow-burning rice,
peach petals quiver over silver tray.

# TO GET OVER YOU

Ever hear a long summer story
street hard against your face

that skirt is the perfect cut
how did your ass get so nice

will you torture me for hours
I love inflatable mattresses

now Chanel and cigarettes
make me want to drink blood

here is the last stanza it's not
romantic I hope your boss

realizes your time is valuable
and pays you more money soon.

# COBBLER

Your family is from Russia
for generations
they molded the soles
of shoes, laced
leather with necks bent
amid arcane tools,
shelves steeped
and tables crowded.
You raise an eye to passerby
for a second
then return to craft a fit,
to form with fingers
useful furniture for feet.
If you can make a pair
that doesn't hurt,
I'll visit your shop forever.

# MONUMENTS AFTER MIDNIGHT

The 7 train is down which leaves the E—
outside Grand Central at Cipriani
the party continues, there's enough cash
to go round, let's get a drink.

The Yale Club hosted a benefit
tonight, they likely raised a record.
Vanderbilt is dark after midnight
so over to Fifth, chocolate and watches

with saints on gilt doors, Atlas has a ball,
I've been here before, Mom and Dad
for brunch at the Rainbow Room,
with money you can name your street!

Fitzgerald spoke of a dream
so close we can hardly fail to grasp—
I see the green light, descend subway stairs,
rose petals scattered on a platform floor.

# SATURDAY

Traffic on the expressway
like wind on water,
days to weekend.
Drunken instances
are forgotten.
Water absolves all,
wind touches all,
all escapes.
I want it over.
Friday felt like shit—
mindless human beings,
mind openings.
Dark bars are the same
and darker ones
disappear.
In the morning song,
oatmeal, hot water,
you can be you
the words will come
I think it's fine
vehicles shake the building.

# GALAMITES

Sometimes a prayer persists beyond answer,
circles in the afterdark, a lone player
     reasons with love—
appetitive glow, champagne, filet
     on a billionaire's table,
he envisions life below as lived above,
bright lights fade for all to see,
     paddles in the air
recited slowly for the room to hear,
calm ballroom, dessert served,
the gathering is for people to share—
backstage exit to a horse-drawn carriage,
     street moist with night
to simply roam, take the train home,
settle back, reflect on past career and future.

# VIEW FROM BROOKLYN

Manhattan martyr do not spare your life
for material possibility attracts
the manifesting spirit of this age,
mechanic clash,
barrage of modern things
obscuring what was
once native isle,
still raw, still mystical—

tunnels through night toward destiny
unknown yet there shoot
vessels on the brink of rough repose,
two rivers spent in a haze of morning
laser an epithet from centuries
before the present era;

tigers of immortal blood
charge limits
none can foretell,
a future fortune
awaits your arrival—

indigenous people, we have made
your land urban imagery,
speculated and paved stone surfaces,
built taller edifice for generations
to explain, monuments of hardest work,
vehicles combust;

>—→

saddle steel,
recycle energy, burn oil, electricity
and blast tomorrow
to get there faster...
notice anything in the noise
as airplanes streak the sky
with fecund messages and war continues?

# VERY ADULT

Now I'm in the city
at my apartment
Saturday night
having a beer
pistachios and piano
leaning on this
blue-legged table
nearer by train
yet still without you.

# THE OPERA

How many radio frequencies traverse
the fibrous delay of space,
coliseum of panacea, music bold—
people crowd a florid stage
to hear the world sing,
we applaud the pain, intermission
champagnes the ceiling,
calm balcony, cathartic urban flood;
I see no street but grassy lawn,
children run, a fountain
of fresh spring water flings diamonds
to the sun—bells announce
Act Two, the crystal gets quaffed,
we shuffle to transitory chairs,
face deliriums of blood,
passion's perfume, then die extreme.

# FRANK'S GRANDCHILDREN

They're pretty hot and read
with remarkable aplomb
(like poetry matters)
in Brooklyn.
They recount
urban escapades
with deadpan serendipity
to wine-starved rooms
of immigrants.
I don't fuck with them
but would like to.
Some escaped
academic captivity
for real jobs,
travels, and post online.
I love them
and lead the lucky
to his grave:
"Grace to have lived
as variously as possible."

# DRUMMERS

Two men in Union Square
duel with worn
drumsticks
on five gallon buckets,
architecture echoes
their anger,
muscle machine of society,
hearts bounce
window to window,
metal bells burst
the energy.
They tap a rising tempo
together, succeed
in capturing the crowd's
attention, and dollars
flow in their empty buckets.

# FATHER DEMO

April pigeons peck the rain-wet square,
Japanese Zelkovas bloom chartreuse,
dates resume, pizza in the piazza,
the neighborhood guys work something out,
newspapers, dogs and salads appear;

Our Lady of Pompeii is here to stay
another twenty years. Once photographs
were printed out to share with friends, get doubles
we would say, drunk in the shade, youthful, free
as pigeons skirt fountain lips a priest
claimed there's no dilemma too great for time
to heal, the right action is none, we sit
together on spaceship benches,
survivors one and all from foreign lands.

A stranger on the street
  said what was in my head;
She spoke the words I thought
  before they were released.

# LONG ISLAND CITY

Mountain like buildings,
glass and steel to misty canopies of cloud,
an elevated train turns the corner
and squeals to a stop,
traffic ramps the Queensboro Bridge,
wraps my building in symphony—
constant pavement, tires,
trucks and trains
transporting thousands by the second,
glimmering airplane lights,
skyline window views,
the low stars,
miasma of yellow, white and blue
flickering, bold billboards
hung from the track advertise films and soda,
silver ribbon of river,
slick sheen of the Chrysler Building,
island between rivers,
a long line of solid shapes stacked in air
with millions inside—
the love and dying in our city,
wine by the water tower,
all the signs, graffiti covered walls,
taxi parking lots, strip bars, restaurants,
subway stops, sirens, and new construction.

# SUNDAY

High, high, high buildings
climb the ocean sky,
far more stars than grains
of sand, once oysters
were big as basketballs,
land cheap as nuts—
invest it in New York
for returns, instant futures.
Who can grasp a dream
on the pavement,
who plopped old temples
on skyscrapers? Steam
clouds water tower roofs,
winter wind whistles
in forty-fifth story windows.

# MANHATTAN, 2003

Leave nothing undescribed, surrounding I
were caves and artificial corridors
into night, convex passage
through steel and concrete vein,
a lot was lost—
homeward, platform
under pavement crowned by silver mien,
us carefree ones regaled
mad tales of yesterday and sang
conglomerates yet built, empiric things,
raged to urinate
on militant morals
held as statute carnage for the world,
we witnessed it do war not brace mankind;
skyscraping laughter fell from high
my friends, no western horizon.

# TAILOR

Spin me a velvet tuxedo
to dazzle the crowd,
jettison frugality,
make it lavish—
spools of thread
for clothes
draped wall to wall,
furnish the flesh,
sew rainbows around
torso, leg and arm.
The needle pierces
a new garment,
door swings, bell rings.
I'll vaunt your talent
online to others,
and post photos of this.

# FEDERAL HALL

Washington watches Wall St. from a pedestal,
     the graffiti is gone, strike at the source
of myths and they evaporate, pillars crumble,
     people separate, and resilience rises.

A hound howls in the emptiness that was history,
     suffering and strife, our legacy transformed
Manhattan into capital architecture, downtown
     towers scale the sky, and tempt mortality.

It all started here—first congress, first freedoms,
     first president to represent the new ideal,
hard to uphold, those patrons of justice raised
     their eyes to a society of masterful people.

A goose honks that this is no nation of solitude
     but a bombastic majority of friends, unruly,
peaceful, built for joy, money and experiments,
     to turn nothing to something, dreams to reality.

# THE CITY VOLCANIC

I search the streets and park
for evidence beyond time,
invisible spirits deliver
messages from the dead.

Maybe souls are contained
and feel the separation
of many becoming one,
spreading outward.

Maybe souls contain
elements that stir and fly
to various points,
and nourish life's richness.

Maybe heat, light, sound
form rivers of energy
and people pass unaware
the brilliant power of creation.

Maybe stone, steel, glass
all have unknown properties
that transfer energy
to converse with people.

# CHANEL AND CIGARETTES

What's this talk about death?
I haven't done it yet.
There's something sticky
on the table I don't
know what it is.
Nothing more to appreciate.

# THIS COSMIC MIRACLE

I see in the city, vast and out of control,
a molecular strand like growth
indifferent to destiny,
ten million people each night
ever changing—
shapes of buildings rearrange the sky,
clouds cling, rivers thread islands,
supple boughs protrude
from maximum blocks of concrete,
glass and steel mushrooms,
architectural air,
digital maps tell us where to go.
I see from street to park,
days lost in reflection
on the grass, a bus of gloom,
memories return
in a song from someone's window,
laundry, liquor, nail shops—
the endless list walking a single block
at six o'clock vaping
in a tobacco shop,
there used to be one of you
now there are two.
I see styles unveiled each fashion week,
villages plundered by drunks
at night, little order to the chaos
yet all fulfilled.
I see the cap off a fire hydrant
and children splash
the deliberately free water of New York.

# CIUDAD NUEVA

A water fountain plumes for all to taste
moments together only last so long,
remember the High Line opera,
it seemed to take hours
to find our way...
       the new city arose from trains,
Hudson Yards never had a care now gobs
of people stroll there, Vessel twisting dreams
outside the Shed and images of Spain,
enough to sell at auction—
experience supreme, for the world
loves an amplified conclusion,
human attractions take center stage,
the highest outdoor skydeck in the West
surveys New Jersey, from ashes come wings.

# GOOD THINGS

To start with, I made it through
a routine morning,
walked to the dry cleaner
without any trousers
admired my legs
with a woman in an SUV
(fresh air, the stink)
and read how everything
is meaningless, like a dream.
Nothing is real
least of all heartache,
rode the subway thinking
once you've learned
to love death
with your whole heart
you are free.
Walking to my office
a familiar homeless beggar
on the corner
Mario the doorman said
there are so many good things.

# QUOINS

A bus in the fog on Friday
tunnels toward the city.

Third Avenue is festival loud,
people exit buildings,
airborne debris, doormen
guard elevators to the rooftop.

Dinner, skylights hip
the panorama, fluted pilasters;
sausage, vegetables steam,
bitter arugula, pop of tomato.

A glass of wine on the edge,
buildings block stars
across the street,
bass turns night to dream.

# STATIONS

Thanks to the one
who lets us go
wherever—
foot traffic flows
up and down
long halls,
underground odors,
platforms
empty and fill.
Shoes march
the solid
rough wet cement.
Echoes screech
off beam,
parallel steel rails,
black holes,
vessels depart
not always on time.
May your travels
lead to wealth
and serve
those who
don't have enough.

# THE PENTHOUSE

If the ceiling is high and marble walls
adorned with tapestries sown
for battle and romance,
ornate furniture decorates the room,
antiques remember history
with immediate beauty,
a chandelier nests in gold fixture,
candles glow in sconces, a red carpet
and pillows, plush bedspread,
the grand mattress, curtains drape
the window street view,
cosmopolitans shop for gifts
to express their feelings, holiday spirits
gather to make life more bearable.

# OVER THE QBP

Expect the 7 train to slow
　　at Queensboro Plaza
and construction to block
　　your downtown view.

One day the sky promotes
　　supertall skyscrapers
and circling birds witness
　　the river catastrophe.

In evening airplanes sail
　　a blood gold sunset
while high inside towers
　　people search for life.

# THE SUPREME POEM

The voice said if you go now you will have
        the meat for poetry
And there it was, alive, the voice right
About it via psychic connectivity.

There is no coincidence—
There is higher awareness, holy images,
        the world is holy.

Here's a glimpse of the supreme poem:
A train stops its electric motion,
Passengers leap from closing doors,
        dash through turnstiles,
The crowd moves up and down
        escalators and stairs,
Pigeons clap their busy wings
And someone lies on the sidewalk.

There are many stations—
It cannot be captured with cameras,
It cannot be captured with microphones.

Now try to say goodbye,
And turn from the one you love the most.

# EDITING

The gradual ascent of buildings
like a staircase in the sky,
stone arch bent spine,
penthouse patio,
the ventilation steam—
someone else's apartment,
a spiritual high,
the bold climb windows
to certain vantage,
shimmering moments of life
endure fallen light,
cold air cracks
a thermodynamic explosion,
mug of hot water,
kefir on granola,
and poetry manuscript by Esther.

# REMNANTS

I see your face
above sidewalks
tree and gate
everything different
everything digital
stone lion on the fence
person coughing
behind the colonnade
snow, limb, bone.

Rain gushes from a gutter under the BQE.
A leak in the ceiling, everything's
not okay, but there's a pot
to catch the water.
Four days ago goodbye. Three days ago
a dumpster by the building.
Two days ago someone made
a costly mistake.
Then Franco left the window open.
I woke up angry.
They did not know what they did.
The one who loves more
becomes happy like never before.
I live in a gritty, shitty city.
I love you bent over the fire escape
as people watch from cars and neighbors
turn on their lights at 3.00 am.
Yesterday miserable poems
came from the printer
I laughed at the leaky architecture
and James Baldwin
said 'I'll show you how to find the moon.'

# BARTENDERS

They shift and turn in unison,
dancing in a drunk ballet.

Candlelight flickers,
bottles gleam green and gold,
and music, source unseen,
fills the ample cavern.

There are televisions
with movies and shows,
news from outside—
games, fights, happenings.

The bartenders serve
the hungry, the sad, the lovers.

Once upon the Oak Bar we drank martinis
as horse-drawn carriages rang
the Plaza steps, before Central Park South
turned billionaire's row, we napped
off hangovers by booksellers
who make Grand Army continental,
gala-goers marched stone walls
laid by hand, many moons—
now city planners frame the land
beyond imagination, who can guess
what supertalls predict?
I remember our afternoon siesta
before the Jitney came, heartbreak express,
an endless softball game with friends.

# WHY FALL?

The improbable stupidity of love
turns light and playful boys
into kneeling men. Why fall?
Patterns are nice, but still.

Men spit on one side of the street
as women hum on the other,
animal thrill of crossing
over, what has fallen is the case.

# HAPPY PLACE

Still quiet dock on tidal estuary,
island skyline changing with regularity,
helicopters surf the wind,
a ferry plows ahead.
The spot young lovers kiss outdoors
on picnic tables—bare elbows
plastic cups of beer
plates of grilled meat
with hot sauce.
It's summer, technicians
survey the new headquarters,
I'll retreat to beaches
to watch more gradual destruction,
the rising water
gallops shoreward oblivious.
Will the future thank us or earth sink?
Architects know
the best thing to do is just love
one another imperfectly.
Things will never be the same,
a boat with a billboard
trolls the luminous
and gray river,
I'm in a tower overlooking everything,
young lovers know the way.

# GOLD STREET

To live at the level of dreams, the top floor
of imagination, where stone wings
emerge from scaffolding, fly the cold air
through metamorphic light,
and reach high temple.
Pillars encircle everything,
a lone helicopter hovers in the sky—
clear victory, direct ascent, everlasting life.

I fly on wings of imagination
to meet the reality
of her gaze. The mad
storm gates,
museums
keep them out.
Her eyes complete
what they see. The mad
write poems
with bittersweet
love for stranger and friend
alike. She sits
on a marble bench
to adjust a boot
and artwork floods the palace.

# THE UMBRELLA

Under an awning the ineffable figure paused,
A person full of meaning, no mirage,
        spirit unlike any other.

Her bronze eyes spot the window mannequin,
        dim behind its glass,
Apparition in a dress, lean and elegant
        amid urban ambiance.

A decade passes.
Suddenly rain pummels the pavement,
        an umbrella opens,
Her reflection grows a widespread dome,
The gray street and sky disappear.

        Quick faces eyes cannot pierce,
        exotic taps on the sidewalk,
        rapid acceleration on car hood
           and garbage can,
        water gushes from gutters
        and spills into the sewer grate.

Her calm expression of surprise,
Where did it go, really, she smiles, where?

# BALLERINA

A dancer leaps
into life
certain of life,
touches
and lets go—
movement is all
there is, once again.

# HUDSON RIVER PARK

I think across the water is another world,
another reality, another version of life
where time does not exist.
Bells shiver in their Byzantine tower,
my heart stops love's seizure,
a sailboat passes between two shores,
sunlight feathers the cloud,
moment upon moment
builds a reflection
on the cool, polluted river—
nothing is better than Sundays with you.

# BEST ALIVE

You come to the city,
rendezvous at a bar
in college colors
and accept praise
like a sincere actor.

Come back, come back
dear one return—
I cannot go.

Favorite muse is subtle
for *La Bohème*
the moment lives
forever, I revel
in it perched on
the third ring forever.

Come back, come back
good one return—
I won't forget.

You are an aria whose
lyrics fill my soul
with applause
none can reproduce,
you are absolute.

→

Come back, come back
fair one return—
I cannot go.

Friends, lovers, partners
we are nothing
but separate
people unconnected
even so my heart
calls you Queen of Love.

Come back, come back
dear one return—
the peace you know.

We eat Moroccan food
and speak of plans
walking through the park,
infinite lights spark
your eye, spirited one,
the universe
appears to condense
the best alive inside you.

Come back, come back
good one return—
I cannot go.

>——→

If you stand by a window
the world will end
well, your body
is a statue,
your voice is charm,
your hand graces
the skin of my memory.

Come back, come back
fair one return—
I won't forget.

Perfect, true, dull words,
elegant and wild
describe you,
many call me a liar
yet I don't exaggerate,
no one will ever
persuade me otherwise.

Come back, come back
dear one return—
I cannot go.

# VISION

Like that energy shifts,
summer, cold front,
September air,
I see it differently—
blurred by adjustment,
one day the way it is.

# BIRDS

It's neither performance nor poetry
jackhammer in the morning
don't let the air in here.
It's a dreary autumn
football and oysters are nice,
champagne too.
Where would you like to go?
I want to walk
down strange alleys
to watch dirty stars above the city.
When birds sing
and love surrounds you
your hair makes me sing too.

# AT THE POETRY BROTHEL

I stare at the chandelier
and drink my first beer in a month
recalling a line from earlier in the night.
Why aren't you here?

Some women wear stockings
one has a long knife in her garter
and blood runs down the leg
let that image go.

You do not care
if someone offers their love
our connection kind of contradicts how
the way I feel about you is over.

# BARBER FOR GIANCARLO

No head was ever
crowned so well.
You cut air,
scissors sculpt,
hands style,
fingers twitch tufts
in a mirror.
The chair spins
a hand dives
past comb,
lotion, oil, salve
to the razor.
You shave my skin,
fashion a look
with a rub
and studious gaze.
Then, like
a bullfighter,
remove the cape.
Here's my tip
with more to come.

# WATERCOLOR

It looks remarkable, utter silhouettes,
dreamy architecture, clear forms

only a hand can imagine, yet eyes
behold things worth religion,

picture of concrete and glass,
intriguing signs, attentive bodies.

Metropolis, metropolis, take my hand,
and reveal a new world tonight.

Your billboards, people on corners
fire escapes and warehouses,

youth, beauty, light on the pavement,
attitude of walkers, street fashions,

pet sniffing air, simultaneous smile
and scowl from pothole, hydrant,

vender, bookshop, bar, sidewalk café,
(a woman in a dark, dirty doorway)

traffic, park, chain link fence, mosque,
a person stands, cyclists peddle past.

People flourish in salon and skyscraper,
in banks, gift shops, and pharmacies.

Tombstones, tombstones superimposed
below big buildings full of lively souls.

# BRONX BOMBERS

The house that Ruth built is no more but boys
still dream of going pro, like everyone else
we took the train to Yankee Stadium
to watch the game,
first glimpse of home, diamond made of dirt,
expansive outfield, advertisements—
who's on the mound and behind the plate?
Hey batter you're on deck, popcorn, peanuts,
cold beer here, splish splash
I was taking a bath,
by the seventh inning stretch, it's One,
Two, Three strikes... watch out for foul balls.

The homeless couple sleeping
in an empty parking spot,
their cardboard bed
exposed to night,
a baby carriage nearby.

# SATURDAY NIGHT

I read books, cheap and easy
like me walking home
from Manhattan
under the BQE (which hangs
over everyone's head)

remembering life
continually passes, traffic,
I was on my phone
more than ever today
and friends liked
some pages and posts.

What's the difference between
the last person you loved
and the last person you'll ever
love? They may not be the same.

Break me on Saturday night
it doesn't take much
love means fuck
but fuck rarely love
and I wait for the words to end.

# LAUNDROMAT

West Indians are the best.
I duck under doors
and dodge silver carts
launched at legs.
Mounds of trousers
and shirts steam.
An old Chinese man
sells soap and softener.
Old magazines
on the folding table.
Clean clothes
for people to claim—
can you fold
this pile while I go
to the grocery?
One day, we'll meet
in Crown Heights
for pumpkin roti my treat.

There is desolation in the industrial night,
  thank you furiously for sparing me
an otherworldly glow—haunted
  by enigmatic principles,
weather storms inside the living soul.

Oh for a fist to hold existence together,
  that doesn't break down doors
for answers but gently, knocks
  on ambiguous tomorrow.
I see the streetlight not too far away.

Here's something random:
  it happens when spring trees flower
from sick nothing in bold display,
  drained spirits refill, and the rest
becomes an offering to you, dearest lovers.

# FOR THANE

You of all singers heard
big rocks beat sirens
poke nightmares
under eyelids,
concrete steel pound
car and truck,
souls carried away
by the river
of dreams,
gutter rain smack
naked streets,
motorcycle screams
along the service road.

# THIS ALL THE TIME

It's time for holiday retreats, to go
from feast to feast, December has a way
of getting us a table with friends,
the days are short and everything depends
on office parties, wearing green or red,
whether to travel home again
(I cannot say what's best for you to do).
The Rockefeller Christmas tree
for tourists to relate, pre-war free heat
might shut off on its own, yet sales
will never cease despite true poverty—
    America is united by a storm,
the weather woman cannot be ignored.

# EAST RIVER

I remember Midwestern plains, country attire,
and promise in my chest to voice
the glorious presence of green imaginations,
turning from the past to face a certain
sunrise on the East River,
light plays in the water off Pier 17,
I dream a new reality;

The Atlantic is cold
as other worlds,
broken glass
gets smashed back
into oblivion,
in our country
anything can happen.

When I return to the East River,
near urban incubators, to watch fortunate
people walk to work on remarkable pavement,
not miniscule, but colossal geometry
guards Manhattan island,
emptiness gets braced, and light in the water
brightens my early morning promenade.

# DEFLATED

The cat clawed my air mattress
a temporary bed, waters
of happiness flow
like ease behind effort,
like sun through torn plastic
on worn linoleum.

This is a launch pad tomorrow
should be better, dust
and hair gather
around cardboard boxes
that are my closet,
and a pickle jar is the toilet.

# TUNNELS IN THE NIGHT

Traffic flows in and out of itself with effervescent fluidity,
Wheels weave paths on stretches of asphalt plateau,
A white dotted line suggests the way to go—
    the yellow smooth in its curvature
Around every bend, true its lead again and again.

I drive through tunnels in the night,
Three dimensional corridors, sitting suspended,
    pedals purchase the floor
With traction for gravity, lights float above
Like delicate candy moons, such precious pearls aloft.

Why speed and chance the alignment of holy vertebrae,
    the serpent neck and skull erect
To the dance of explosive pistons and exhaust?
Her name is Blessing, her heart like a hand dips in life,
Her blood is love, her love is light—Blessing is her name.

# FISH MARKET

Where's the fishmonger?
Fresh catch on display
their shiny scales
outstretched, fins hold
sword and armor,
caught in a busy market,
meat worth its weight.
Once sleek shapes
swam the sea,
gleam icy slopes
under artificial light
nestled stomach to back.
I'll take cod for four
to go with peas,
potatoes, and champagne
for newlywed friends.

# GREENPOINT BLUES

Ignite the dust for powder burns
and dog hair sheds downstairs,
people on the street ache
for country air—a garbage truck
turns the potholed corner
then slam goes
the dumpster's full weight;
"If I hear that one more time,"
Fred says, "I'll go fucking insane."

# THE HOLIDAYS

This is a call to observe
something different.
Pine needles fall
from the evergreen,
lights of time
accelerate with age.
It's a season to repair,
when mist rolls
clouds of mint
in the dead flowers,
and things happen again.

A dandy got his bust in the park
now how's that make you feel on a Sunday
in December? Jazz trio, Christmas carols,
people walking dogs or each other—
it's standard for the wise
to hold the hand of a higher power.
A bicycle wheels past, front tire in the air,
a nonchalant car horn resumes its pigeon
scattering blast in the snowflakes,
quiet anticipation dying
for a purpose, soap bubbles float and burst
before the arch, jazz is right,
a surrealist poet once ascended it
to protest a war that few remember.

# SOLITUDE

I miss the elegance
of joy and hurt to be human
in public spaces,
then go to a party alone.

# SKATERS

Fresh in relationships
they skate hand in hand,
blade frozen water,
shave ice flakes
from a seasonal pond.
Clouds of breath,
crisp steel notes,
a vaulted turn,
thighs pump in unison.
The glassy rink
whistles at winter flight
and I, ringmaster,
call on winter
to keep a flame alive.
Come spring, let
them moisten the buds
of further intimacy.

# FROM NEW JERSEY

Totem lights break on looking back
at things before the night,
river water ice reflecting beams,
clear pillars of light
melting from bank to bank,
elevating a frozen field,
relative columns, edifice composed
of dreamy architecture—
the drive of friendship to a bridge
past Grant's tomb,
cylinders expanding, ever glazed
as frosty beacons white beside the dark.

*Acknowledgements:*

Charles Antin, Tom Arnott, Thane Boulton, Brooklyn Bridge Park Conservancy, The Bumbys, Cael, Ben Cawiezell, Cole, Christina Daigneault, Ben Fama, Paul Florez, David Lynch Foundation, East End Hospice, Jesse Elliott, Karen Hershey, Sarah Jones, Madeleine, Mirrorball, Mom & Dad, Jeffrey Nolte, Murat Oztaskin, Larry Rundie, Harry Santa-Olalla, Richard Saudek, CK Swett, Val & Chad, and Joanna C. Valente.

Thank you Simon Van Booy for years of love, respect & support.

CPSIA information can be obtained
at www.ICGtesting.com
Printed in the USA
BVHW041204120522
636875BV00013B/209/J